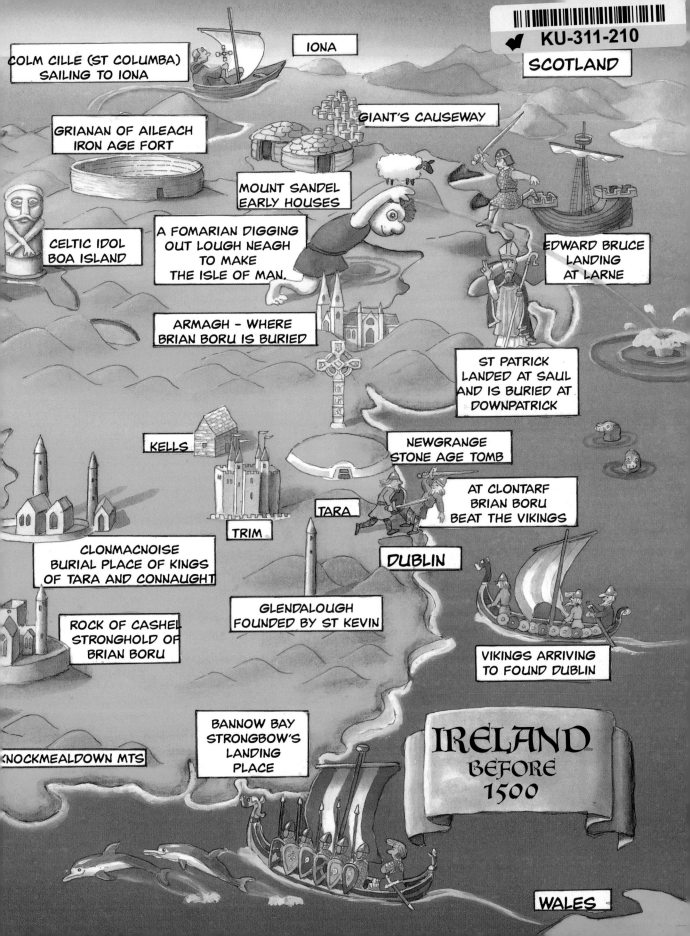

COLM CILLE (ST COLUMBA) SAILING TO IONA

IONA

SCOTLAND

GRIANAN OF AILEACH IRON AGE FORT

GIANT'S CAUSEWAY

MOUNT SANDEL EARLY HOUSES

CELTIC IDOL BOA ISLAND

A FOMARIAN DIGGING OUT LOUGH NEAGH TO MAKE THE ISLE OF MAN.

EDWARD BRUCE LANDING AT LARNE

ARMAGH – WHERE BRIAN BORU IS BURIED

ST PATRICK LANDED AT SAUL AND IS BURIED AT DOWNPATRICK

KELLS

NEWGRANGE STONE AGE TOMB

TARA

AT CLONTARF BRIAN BORU BEAT THE VIKINGS

TRIM

DUBLIN

CLONMACNOISE BURIAL PLACE OF KINGS OF TARA AND CONNAUGHT

ROCK OF CASHEL STRONGHOLD OF BRIAN BORU

GLENDALOUGH FOUNDED BY ST KEVIN

VIKINGS ARRIVING TO FOUND DUBLIN

KNOCKMEALDOWN MTS

BANNOW BAY STRONGBOW'S LANDING PLACE

IRELAND BEFORE 1500

WALES

# The Story of IRELAND

Told by Richard Brassey and Stewart Ross
Illustrated by Richard Brassey

Orion Children's Books
*and*
Dolphin Paperbacks

*For Judith and Paul*

R B

*To Chess*

S R

First published in Great Britain in 2001
by Orion Children's Books/Dolphin Paperbacks
a division of the Orion Publishing Group Ltd,
5 Upper St Martin's Lane, London WC2H 9EA

Text © Richard Brassey and Stewart Ross 2001
Illustrations © Richard Brassey 2001

A catalogue record for this book is available from the British Library.

Printed in Italy by Printer Trento S.r.l.

ISBN 1 85881 848 6 (HB)
ISBN 1 85881 849 4 (PB)

**M**illions of years ago all the land on earth was stuck together in one huge super-continent called Pangaea. Ireland was right in the middle . . . at the very centre of the world!

But during the time of the dinosaurs, Pangaea slowly split into smaller pieces. Ireland found itself, covered in ice, at the top left-hand corner of the bit called Europe.

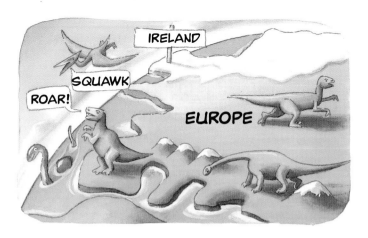

Eventually things warmed up but before the ice completely melted and filled the Irish Sea, many animals moved in. About 9,000 years ago the first people walked across from Scotland. The snakes, however, left it too late!

The round huts which once stood at Mount Sandel may have been the first houses built in Europe.

I WENT HUNTING TODAY. HOW ABOUT YOU?

FISHING!

For thousands of years people lived by hunting and fishing until about 3500 BC when farmers paddled over from Britain.

As well as farming they brought many new skills such as pottery and cloth-making. But they were best at making tombs.

AND I'LL EVEN THROW IN A 5,000 YEAR GUARANTEE!

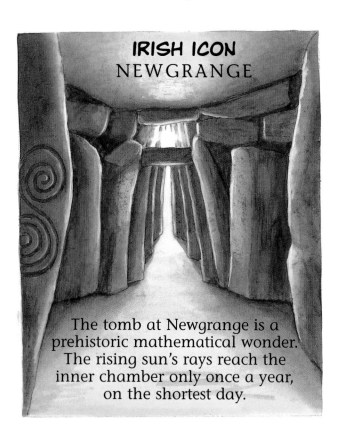

**IRISH ICON**
NEWGRANGE

The tomb at Newgrange is a prehistoric mathematical wonder. The rising sun's rays reach the inner chamber only once a year, on the shortest day.

AN-BHLASTA!

SLÀINTE

The next settlers were good at working with soft metals like bronze, gold and silver.
Most present-day Irish and the Irish language are probably descended from these 'Beaker People'.

The next lot, known as Celts, began arriving around 600 BC. Their way of living soon got mixed up with everybody else's to become what is known as 'Gaelic' culture. By now people had started making things out of iron.

There were four main kingdoms and about 150 smaller ones, all constantly quarrelling. Their kings (or *rí*) built thousands of stone hill forts. Others felt safer living in lake villages called crannogs.

The Romans took a look at Ireland but decided not to try to conquer it.

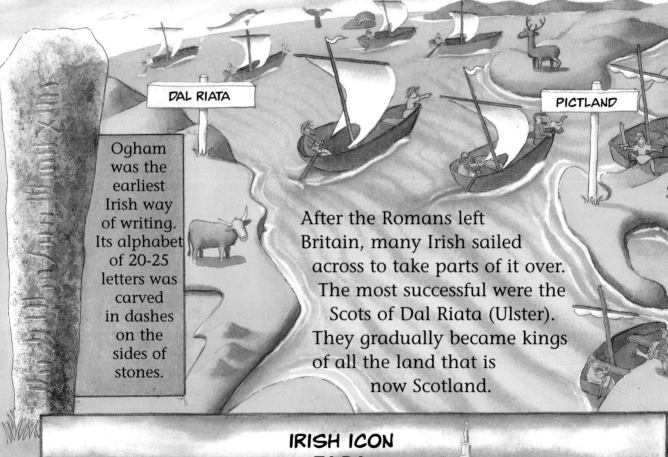

Ogham was the earliest Irish way of writing. Its alphabet of 20-25 letters was carved in dashes on the sides of stones.

After the Romans left Britain, many Irish sailed across to take parts of it over. The most successful were the Scots of Dal Riata (Ulster). They gradually became kings of all the land that is now Scotland.

**IRISH ICON**
TARA

'The sacred space', seat of mighty Lugh and the kings of ancient mythology, became a symbol of Irish nationhood.
It has served as an important meeting point throughout history.

No one is quite sure how and when Christianity came to Ireland. St Patrick, from Britain, is the best known of several missionaries. The Irish accepted Christianity with a will. Their conversion is said to have taken place without a single martyrdom. For 300 years Irish monasteries and learning were the wonder of Europe.

## IRISH ICON
### BOOK OF KELLS

This copy of the Gospels was probably begun on the island of Iona and finished in the monastery of Kells. Hand-written, lavishly illustrated and decorated, it is one of the masterpieces of the Western world.

Irish missionaries and scholars travelled all over Europe, from Scotland to Russia. They were so well educated that the saying went: "If a man knows Greek he must be Irish!"

THEY MUST BE IRISH

καλημερα!

γεια αου!

St Patrick is famous for chasing the snakes from Ireland. He cunningly lured the last old serpent into a box and threw it in the sea. Nice story but not true – see page 3!

I BET THAT BOX ISN'T BIG ENOUGH FOR ME.

GET IN AND I'LL PROVE TO YOU IT IS!

## IRISH ICON
### SKELLIG MICHAEL

The monks who lived in beehive-shaped huts, perched high on Skellig rock in the stormy Atlantic, chose a hard, lonely life of prayer and fasting

Old Gaelic customs lived on. No court was complete without its file, or poet, to sing of the past and comment on the present.

Everyone had an exact position in society – freemen were divided into 27 classes. Although the church didn't approve, divorce was allowed and the rich could have several wives.

Money did not exist so cows were normally used instead.

From the 790s hordes of plundering Vikings arrived. Later they came to settle, and their bases – Dublin, Limerick, Cork and Wexford – grew into the first towns. They also introduced money!

By the 11th century the Viking lands were part of the patchwork of kingdoms struggling to outdo each other.

Brian Boru emerged as the strongest king. At the famous Battle of Clontarf (1014) he defeated the Viking Dubliners and the Leinstermen, who had joined together to defend themselves. He himself was killed.

## BRIAN BORU
## (940-1014)

King of Munster and the first non-Neill to claim the High Kingship. A fine soldier and keen politician, he kept on good terms with the church.

IT'S THE HIGH KING OF ALL IRELAND ... KNEEL!

IT'S O'NEILL TO YOU!

The Uí Neill had become the most powerful family in Ireland. Some of them claimed to be 'King of All the Irish' when in fact they did not rule all the Uí Neill.

By now the powerful monasteries of the Irish church seemed old-fashioned. New customs were introduced from Europe, bishops got more power and the church was united under the Archbishop of Armagh.

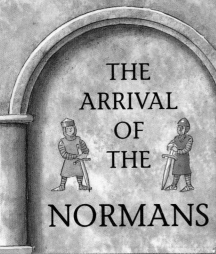

# THE ARRIVAL OF THE NORMANS

The Pope wanted the High King to support church reforms but he couldn't work out which king was High King. So he said Henry II of England could be in charge.

Three years earlier King Dermot of Leinster had run off with the wife of King Tiernan, his neighbour. Tiernan drove Dermot from Ireland. Dermot went to Henry II for help. Henry was too busy.

But some of his Norman barons, led by Strongbow, Earl of Pembroke, agreed to lend Dermot a hand.

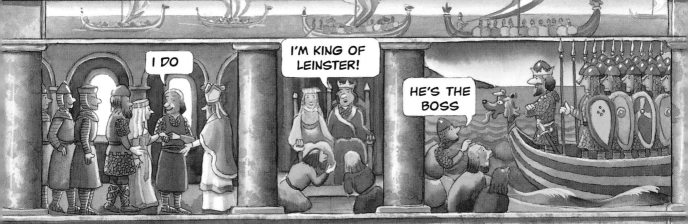

They soon conquered half the country and Strongbow married Dermot's daughter, Aoife. When Dermot died, Strongbow called himself King of Leinster.

He was clearly getting too big for his boots. So Henry popped over with a huge army and all the Normans and many Irish kings agreed he was boss.

Ireland had no answer to the Norman war machine. The High King, Rory O'Connor, gave in and accepted Henry II as his overlord. The invaders went on seizing land until they controlled most of the country.

Energetically they set about changing everything. A governor, called 'justiciar', ruled Ireland for the absent king. It was divided into counties and manors under local lords. A fair system of justice, called Common law, was introduced and in 1264 the first Irish parliament met.

Many new towns sprang up. Large solid castles and cathedrals towered over the land.

Communication was not always easy.

**IRISH ICON**
TRIM CASTLE

The largest stone castle in the country was built beside the River Boyne by Walter de Lacy. At one time Trim nearly became the capital.

11

The barons brought English servants and priests. Merchants and craftsmen settled in Ireland too. It was not long before they thought of themselves as Irish rather than English.

**IRISH ICON**
GLENDALOUGH

The monastery in the Wicklow Mountains, founded by St Kevin, was a popular pilgrimage centre for nine hundred years until destroyed in 1398.

The life of ordinary peasants changed little. But the upper classes had lost land, power and prestige. In 1258 Brian O'Neill – last King of Tara – led a rebellion. He was defeated and his head was sent as a present to Henry III in England.

Fed up with the English King, Irish leaders invited King Haakon of Norway and, later, Edward Bruce (brother of Scotland's Robert) to take his place. Haakon never got round to it. Edward was crowned king but then killed in battle.

By 1300 the English grip was weakening. Some barons felt they had more in common with the Irish than with their distant English king. But the Gaelic chieftains still resented them and hired Scottish soldiers, called Gallowglasses, to win back land they had lost.

The Black Death, which reached Ireland in 1348, wiped out nearly half the population and caused enormous hardship.

When Art MacMurrough declared himself King of Leinster, Richard II was furious. He came over to Ireland and defeated Art. But Art tried again, so Richard made a second visit. In the middle of it he was called back to England in a hurry and murdered. King Art survived.

The 'Old English' Earls of Ormond, Kildare and Desmond had now been settled in Ireland for over two hundred years. They spoke Gaelic and were friends with Gaelic chiefs. The Third Earl of Desmond, known as Gerald the Poet, even wrote verses in Irish. During the fifteenth century the Wars of the Roses kept the English kings busy and one or other of the Earls ran things in Ireland. The Eighth 'great' Earl of Kildare was governor under five kings.

### THE ENGLISH PALE

The Pale was a large fortified area around Dublin, very much like a part of England. Beyond the Pale the 'old English' lords and Gaelic chiefs ran their estates like little kingdoms. Often Gaelic customs survived or were revived.

**IRISH ICON**
BOOK OF BALLYMOTE

This proud collection of information about Gaelic Ireland, including the Ogham alphabet, was written at the end of the 14th century

When Henry Tudor became King of England, he decided it was time to take Ireland in hand.
He sent Sir Edward Poynings to tell parliament that they couldn't meet or pass laws unless he, Henry, said they could.
This was known as Poynings' Law.

His son, Henry VIII, took an even firmer hand. He shut the Ninth Earl of Kildare in the Tower of London. The Earl's son, Silken Thomas, rebelled. Henry had him executed.

Henry now made himself head of the Irish church. He used his power to close nearly half the monasteries and take their lands and wealth.

Henry VIII was the first English king to call himself 'King' of Ireland instead of 'Lord'. He made everyone agree that all the land was his; only those who did agree got their land back.

**HOW TO BECOME AN ENGLISH LORD**

HOPELESS!

BETTER

I SAY! EXCEL-

NOW JUST GIVE US YOUR LAND!

All through the sixteenth century the English tried to make Ireland English. The Gaelic language and dress were outlawed. No one was allowed to be Roman Catholic. Irish chiefs were turned into English-style lords and Irish land was given to English settlers. Such high-handed behaviour led to three great rebellions.

Shane O'Neill, 'the O'Neill', invaded the Pale but was defeated. His head was pickled and sent to Lord Deputy Sidney.

DIE, COUSIN!

James FitzMaurice Fitzgerald led the opposition in Munster but was killed by his own cousin.

DON'T DO IT AGAIN

Hugh O'Neill, Earl of Tyrone, led the 'last great Gaelic counter-attack'. He was beaten at Kinsale but was pardoned.

These were hard times. There are stories of wolves coming down from the hills, and of people eating nettles – and even each other – to stay alive.

**IRISH ICON**
**BLARNEY STONE**

WAFFLE! WAFFLE!

Cormac, Lord of Blarney, was all talk and no action.

BLARNEY! BLARNEY! WHAT HE SAYS HE NEVER MEANS. IT'S THE USUAL BLARNEY!

Queen Elizabeth exploded with rage.

OK, I'LL TALK!

Those who kiss the Stone in Blarney Castle get the gift of the gab like Cormac.

In the mid -16th century the English government decided to encourage English people to come and live in Ireland. They thought it was the only way to make the Catholics behave and speak English. This was called 'Plantation'.

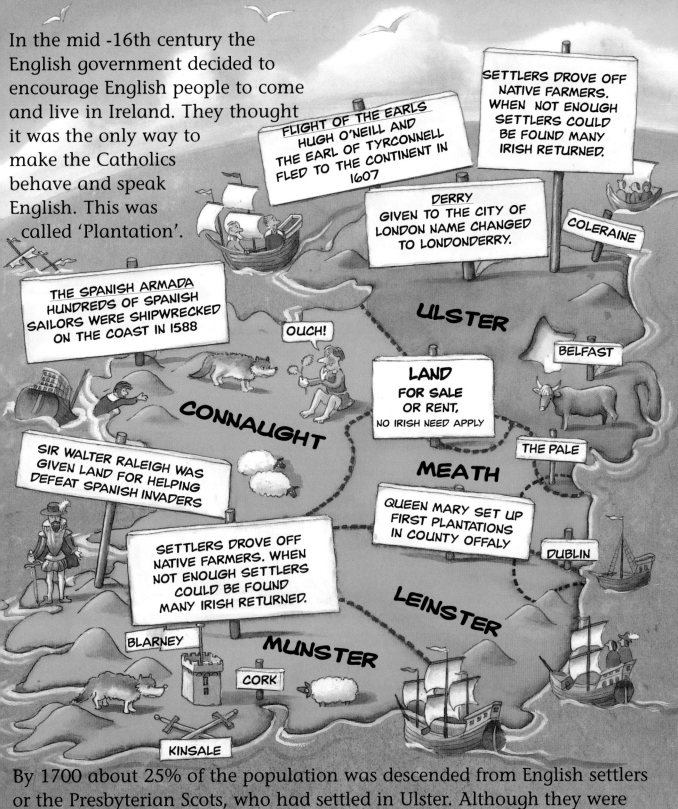

FLIGHT OF THE EARLS HUGH O'NEILL AND THE EARL OF TYRCONNELL FLED TO THE CONTINENT IN 1607

SETTLERS DROVE OFF NATIVE FARMERS. WHEN NOT ENOUGH SETTLERS COULD BE FOUND MANY IRISH RETURNED.

DERRY GIVEN TO THE CITY OF LONDON NAME CHANGED TO LONDONDERRY.

COLERAINE

THE SPANISH ARMADA HUNDREDS OF SPANISH SAILORS WERE SHIPWRECKED ON THE COAST IN 1588

OUCH!

ULSTER

BELFAST

LAND FOR SALE OR RENT, NO IRISH NEED APPLY

CONNAUGHT

SIR WALTER RALEIGH WAS GIVEN LAND FOR HELPING DEFEAT SPANISH INVADERS

MEATH

THE PALE

QUEEN MARY SET UP FIRST PLANTATIONS IN COUNTY OFFALY

DUBLIN

SETTLERS DROVE OFF NATIVE FARMERS. WHEN NOT ENOUGH SETTLERS COULD BE FOUND MANY IRISH RETURNED.

LEINSTER

BLARNEY

MUNSTER

CORK

KINSALE

By 1700 about 25% of the population was descended from English settlers or the Presbyterian Scots, who had settled in Ulster. Although they were much resented, the settlers did improve farming methods. They also founded 23 new towns, including Coleraine and Belfast.

17

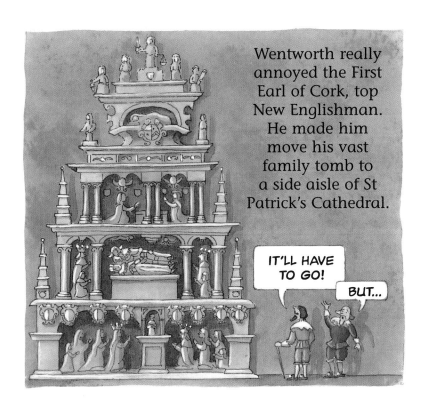

Wentworth really annoyed the First Earl of Cork, top New Englishman. He made him move his vast family tomb to a side aisle of St Patrick's Cathedral.

IT'LL HAVE TO GO!

BUT...

The population was now a fiery mix (see below).

Charles I's tactless Lord Deputy, Governor Thomas Wentworth, managed to annoy just about everyone.

After he was executed, the country exploded into the long, bloody and confusing Confederate War (1641-53).

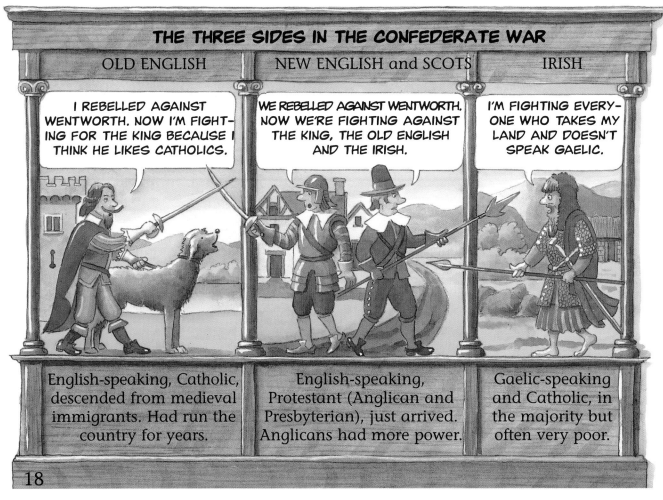

## THE THREE SIDES IN THE CONFEDERATE WAR

| OLD ENGLISH | NEW ENGLISH and SCOTS | IRISH |
|---|---|---|
| I REBELLED AGAINST WENTWORTH. NOW I'M FIGHTING FOR THE KING BECAUSE I THINK HE LIKES CATHOLICS. | WE REBELLED AGAINST WENTWORTH. NOW WE'RE FIGHTING AGAINST THE KING, THE OLD ENGLISH AND THE IRISH. | I'M FIGHTING EVERYONE WHO TAKES MY LAND AND DOESN'T SPEAK GAELIC. |
| English-speaking, Catholic, descended from medieval immigrants. Had run the country for years. | English-speaking, Protestant (Anglican and Presbyterian), just arrived. Anglicans had more power. | Gaelic-speaking and Catholic, in the majority but often very poor. |

In 1649 Oliver Cromwell arrived with his New Model Army. Keen to bring the country firmly under English control once and for all, he teamed up with the Protestants and crushed all opposition. When the people of Drogheda and Wexford were slow to surrender, he broke down the walls and killed many of the inhabitants.

As Catholicism was banned, religious services were held in secret in the open air at 'mass-rocks'.

MASS ROCK

IS THIS DOWN ON THE MAP?

LOOKS LIKE UP TO ME!

Dr William Petty surveyed all the land confiscated by Cromwell. The work was called the 'Down Survey' because he put the results *down* on maps.

## IRISH ICON
### KINSALE

For a time Ireland shared the same government as Britain. Cromwell confiscated his enemies' land (millions of acres) and gave it to his friends and supporters. Their families kept it for over 200 years.

The harbour of this little town, bursting with history, is guarded by the massive star-shaped Charles Fort. Here the English overcame the two earls and their Spanish supporters. James II landed at Kinsale and later fled from here.

19

James II of England was a Catholic. He put the Duke of Tyrconnell in charge and told him to give jobs to Irish Catholics. In 1688 James was thrown out of England and came to Ireland the following year. His daughter Mary and her husband, William of Orange, took over as king and queen.

THE SIEGE OF DERRY

THE BATTLE OF THE BOYNE

Not everyone welcomed James. The Presbyterian apprentice boys shut the gates of Derry. The town held out for 105 days. Then King William arrived and beat James's army on the banks of the Boyne.

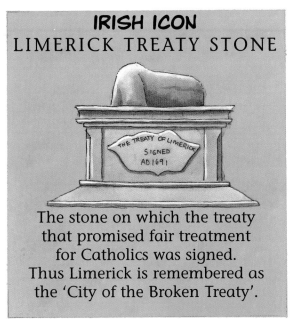

**IRISH ICON**
LIMERICK TREATY STONE

The stone on which the treaty that promised fair treatment for Catholics was signed. Thus Limerick is remembered as the 'City of the Broken Treaty'.

The Treaty of Limerick let Catholic officers leave for the continent (the Flight of the Wild Geese). Catholics were promised toleration, but it never came. Once again the country was under English, Protestant rule.

The Dublin Philosophical Society encouraged people to use science – to make things work better.

GOOD SIR, WHAT IS THE GRADIENT OF THAT DITCH?

?

Harsh laws passed against Catholics said they could not: own weapons; teach; buy land; work for the government or own a horse worth more than £5.

ONLY £4.99 (TAIL EXTRA)

For a while there was peace. Fine buildings were put up, trade grew and population increased. Although English Anglicans made up only 10% of the population, they ran everything, owned nearly all the land and had the best jobs.

FOR EXPORT

Popular Irish exports: linen, wool, leather, lace, soldiers and Catholic priests.

KING, DARLING, COULD MR WOOD MAKE SOME HALFPENNIES FOR IRELAND?

William Wood, a friend of the King's girlfriend, was given the job of making copper coins for Ireland. Nobody in Ireland was asked. There was a huge outcry and Mr Wood was not allowed to do it after all.

## IRISH ICON - CASTLETOWN HOUSE

William Connolly, speaker of the Parliament, built the finest mansion in the country in the style of an Italian palace.

EDMUND BURKE

MARIA EDGEWORTH

**JONATHAN SWIFT WROTE GULLIVER'S TRAVELS**

RICHARD BRINSLEY SHERIDAN

OLIVER GOLDSMITH

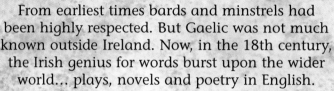

From earliest times bards and minstrels had been highly respected. But Gaelic was not much known outside Ireland. Now, in the 18th century, the Irish genius for words burst upon the wider world… plays, novels and poetry in English.

## IRISH ICON
## GUINNESS

Arthur Guinness established his famous brewery in 1759. It did so well his grandson was able to restore Dublin's St Patrick's Cathedral out of his own pocket.

The Protestant ruling class made sure they were in control. They kept an army of 15,000 men.

But by the middle of the 18th century some 'New English' Protestant 'Patriots' were complaining at the way their country was treated by England. They sympathised with Catholics and said that all people had a right to live under laws to which they had agreed.

Many Scots settlers in Ulster moved on again – this time to the New World.

AMERICA        IRELAND        ENGLAND        FRANCE

Revolution was in the air, first drifting east from America,
then west from France.

THEY DON'T LOOK LIKE BOYS TO ME!

Gangs of men calling themselves 'Whiteboys' protested about bad treatment
by landlords. Catholics and Protestants, feeling threatened by each other,
formed groups called 'Defenders' and 'Peep o' Day Boys'.

WHEN SHALL WE START THE REVOLUTION?

AS SOON AS THE WIND CHANGES!

Wolfe Tone and the United Irishmen wanted Ireland to have a revolution
like the one in France. French ships came to help but were blown home again.
Finally, in 1798 rebellion flared up in several places and was crushed.

In Parliament Henry Grattan
and the Patriot Party called for
Catholics and Protestants to live
in peace and for England to
stop interfering.

This was all too much for the
English government. In 1800
it bullied parliament into passing
an Act of Union and then dissolving
itself. The country was now part
of the United Kingdom.

**IRISH ICON**
BANK OF IRELAND

The headquarters of the
bank is housed in the fine
Old Parliament House, Dublin,
where the Houses of Commons
and Lords sat until done away
with by the Act of Union.

23

## NATIONAL GALLERY OF IRELAND
A treasure house of Irish and European paintings.

## LEINSTER HOUSE
Home of the *Dáil.*

## NATIONAL MUSEUM

## ST STEPHEN'S GREEN
Laid out by Sir Arthur Guinness in 1880. Once site of University College.

## GRAFTON STREET
Fashionable shops, restaurants, cafes, buskers and statue of Molly Malone.

## TRINITY COLLEGE
Home of *The Book of Kells.* Graduates include Bram Stoker *(Dracula)*, Jonathan Swift *(Gulliver's Travels)*, Samuel Beckett *(Waiting for Godot)* and Oscar Wilde.

## LIFFEY

## BANK OF IRELAND

## CUSTOM HOUSE
Said to have been built because a boulder stopped ships reaching the original customs house.

## IRISH ICON
### ABBEY THEATRE

Ireland's national theatre has given the world such masterpieces as J.M. Synge's *Playboy of the Western World* and Sean O'Casey's *The Plough and the Stars.* The original burned down in 1951.

## GENERAL POST OFFICE

## JOYCE'S DUBLIN
Early 20th century Dublin lives on in James Joyce's books. Bloomsday festival is named after one of his characters.

## O'CONNELL STREET
One of the broadest streets in Europe. Statues of O'Connell and Parnell.

24

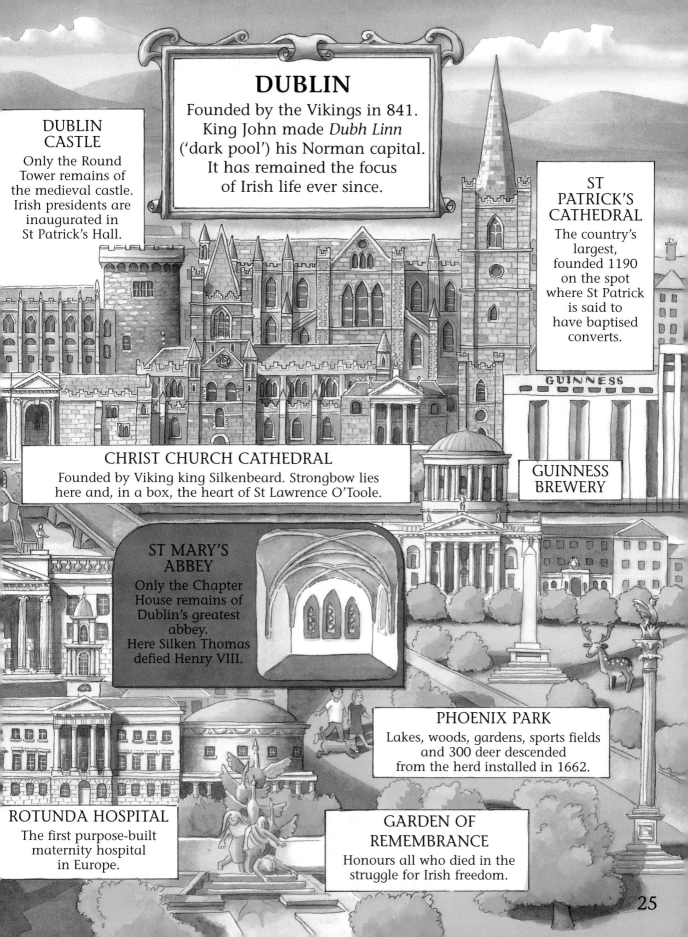

# DUBLIN

Founded by the Vikings in 841. King John made *Dubh Linn* ('dark pool') his Norman capital. It has remained the focus of Irish life ever since.

## DUBLIN CASTLE

Only the Round Tower remains of the medieval castle. Irish presidents are inaugurated in St Patrick's Hall.

## ST PATRICK'S CATHEDRAL

The country's largest, founded 1190 on the spot where St Patrick is said to have baptised converts.

## CHRIST CHURCH CATHEDRAL

Founded by Viking king Silkenbeard. Strongbow lies here and, in a box, the heart of St Lawrence O'Toole.

GUINNESS

## GUINNESS BREWERY

## ST MARY'S ABBEY

Only the Chapter House remains of Dublin's greatest abbey. Here Silken Thomas defied Henry VIII.

## PHOENIX PARK

Lakes, woods, gardens, sports fields and 300 deer descended from the herd installed in 1662.

## ROTUNDA HOSPITAL

The first purpose-built maternity hospital in Europe.

## GARDEN OF REMEMBRANCE

Honours all who died in the struggle for Irish freedom.

25

## THE GREAT FAMINE

IN 1845 THE POPULATION OF IRELAND WAS EIGHT MILLION. POTATOES WERE THE MAIN FOOD.

THAT YEAR AND IN 1846 AND 1848 A FUNGUS RUINED THE POTATO CROP. STARVATION AND DISEASE FOLLOWED. PERHAPS 800,000 PEOPLE DIED. WHOLE VILLAGES WERE DESERTED AS PEOPLE DIED OR EMIGRATED.

In 1839 a hurricane swept through Ireland causing huge damage . . . to some a sign of things to come.

Daniel O'Connell, a lawyer known as 'The Liberator', led the Catholic League to protest for Catholic Rights. Only Protestant MPs had been allowed to sit in the British House of Commons. O'Connell got this changed and was himself elected. He organised huge public protest meetings calling for independence, which alarmed the British government. The 'monster meeting' at Tara was attended by well over half a million people.

Banned Catholic and Nonconformist teachers taught in secret 'hedge schools'.

> 250,000 PEOPLE A YEAR LEFT, MANY FOR THE NEW WORLD. THE GAELIC LANGUAGE AND WAY OF LIFE ALMOST DISAPPEARED. EVEN TODAY THE POPULATION IS ONLY 5,500,000.

> GREEDY LANDLORDS AND THE LONDON GOVERNMENT WERE BLAMED FOR NOT DOING MORE TO HELP.

> THEY'LL HAVE TO SORT IT OUT THEMSELVES.

> FINE. AS LONG AS THEY KEEP PAYING THE RENT.

After the Great Famine three issues held the headlines:

# THE LAND WAR

## Land League leads protests to help small farmers

W. GLADSTONE

British PM gradually gives in to most demands. "My mission is to pacify Ireland," says PM William Gladstone.

NO

**Boycott Boycotted**
Farm labourers refuse to work for Captain Boycott because of unfair treatment. A new word is born.

## THE HOME RULE CAMPAIGN

### Nationalist Party brings House of Commons to a standstill

Party leader, Parnell, refuses to stop talking. Debate lasts all night. British government give in.

CHARLES STEWART PARNELL

VIOLENCE NO ANSWER
Fenians (warriors of ancient Ireland) and Sinn Féin (ourselves) have tried violence but it's getting them nowhere.

# THE UNIONIST THREAT

EDWARD CARSON

## "Ulster will fight, and Ulster will be right!"

So says Edward Carson as Protestant Unionists threaten civil war rather than join a United Ireland. British Conservatives give support.

### WHAT IS THE 'IRISH QUESTION'?

English politicians are complaining that the Irish keep changing the question. "Every time we try to answer, they change it!" said an unnamed backbencher.

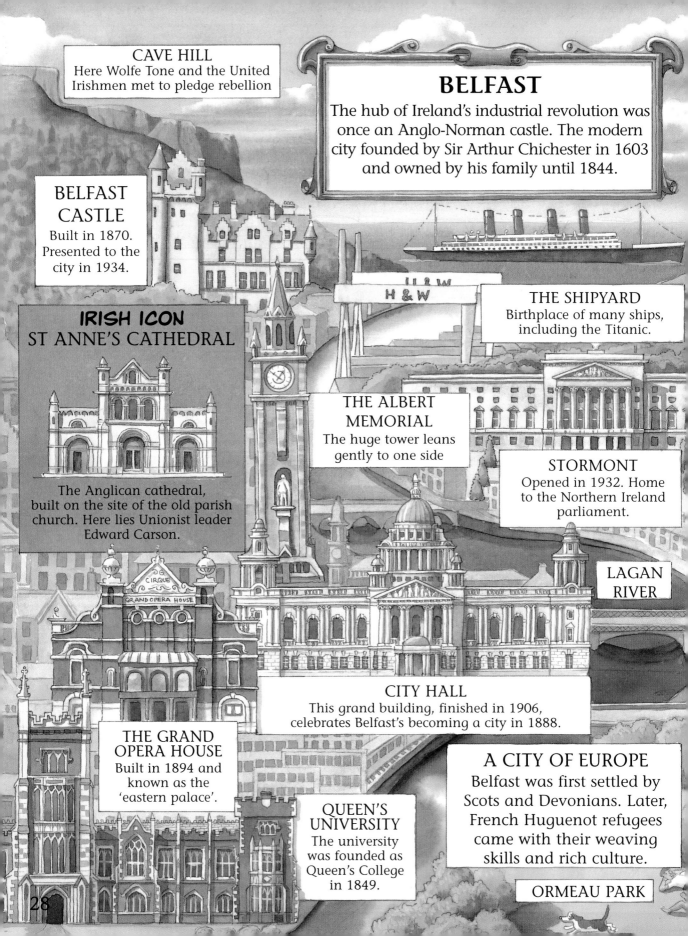

**CAVE HILL**
Here Wolfe Tone and the United Irishmen met to pledge rebellion

# BELFAST
The hub of Ireland's industrial revolution was once an Anglo-Norman castle. The modern city founded by Sir Arthur Chichester in 1603 and owned by his family until 1844.

**BELFAST CASTLE**
Built in 1870. Presented to the city in 1934.

## IRISH ICON
### ST ANNE'S CATHEDRAL
The Anglican cathedral, built on the site of the old parish church. Here lies Unionist leader Edward Carson.

**THE SHIPYARD**
Birthplace of many ships, including the Titanic.

**THE ALBERT MEMORIAL**
The huge tower leans gently to one side

**STORMONT**
Opened in 1932. Home to the Northern Ireland parliament.

**LAGAN RIVER**

**CITY HALL**
This grand building, finished in 1906, celebrates Belfast's becoming a city in 1888.

**THE GRAND OPERA HOUSE**
Built in 1894 and known as the 'eastern palace'.

**QUEEN'S UNIVERSITY**
The university was founded as Queen's College in 1849.

**A CITY OF EUROPE**
Belfast was first settled by Scots and Devonians. Later, French Huguenot refugees came with their weaving skills and rich culture.

**ORMEAU PARK**

THROUGHOUT HISTORY THE IRISH HAVE LOVED HORSES AND HORSE RACING.

NAPOLEON'S HORSE MARENGO WAS IRISH

IN 1752 TWO RIDERS RACED TOWARDS THE STEEPLE OF ST LEGER'S, DONERAILE. STEEPLECHASING HAD BEGUN.

WELCOME TO THE CURRAGH

**IRISH ICON -** THE CURRAGH

These rolling grasslands are the home of the National Stud and the famous racetrack.

In 1893 the Gaelic League *(Conradh na Gaeilge)* was set up to revive the Irish language.

The Gaelic Athletic Association encouraged Irish sport. Members were not allowed to watch 'foreign' games such as cricket and rugby.

DON'T LOOK!

SHEER GENIUS
Irish writers rivalled stout as the country's most famous export.

I HAVE NOTHING TO DECLARE BUT MY GENIUS

ME TOO!

STOUT

GEORGE BERNARD SHAW - PLAYS

WILLIAM BUTLER YEATS    POEMS

OSCAR WILDE    PLAYS

James Joyce    Ulysses

JOHN MILLINGTON SYNGE    THE PLAYBOY OF THE WESTERN WORLD

Sean O'Casey    PLAYS

SAMUEL BECKETT    WAITING FOR GODOT

Although Home Rule had been promised in 1912, it was shelved when the First World War began in 1914. Some nationalists could not wait.

## THE EASTER RISING - 1916

REBELS SEIZED BUILDINGS IN DUBLIN.

MANY WOMEN WERE ACTIVE NATIONALISTS. CONSTANCE MARKIEVICZ WAS THE MOST FAMOUS.

**IRISH ICON**
GENERAL POST OFFICE, DUBLIN

This was the HQ of rebel Irish Volunteers during the Rising.

THE RISING WAS SWIFTLY PUT DOWN BUT THE EXECUTION OF 16 LEADERS TURNED THEM INTO MARTYRS.

In the 1918 elections Unionists, who wanted to stay in the UK, won Ulster. Sinn Féin, who wanted the British out, won the rest. Their MP's refused to go to London and instead they set up the first *Dáil*. The newly formed Irish Republican Army (IRA) attacked the British.

The 'Black and Tans' were half-trained British recruits in police jackets and army trousers.

ULSTER
PART OF U.K.

FREE STATE
FULLY INDEPENDENT

A treaty in 1921 split the country but there were still many who could not accept Ulster staying in the UK as the province of Northern Ireland. For a year there was Civil War.

Finally, in 1937, the fully independent Irish Republic (or Eire) was created under Prime Minister Eamon De Valera.

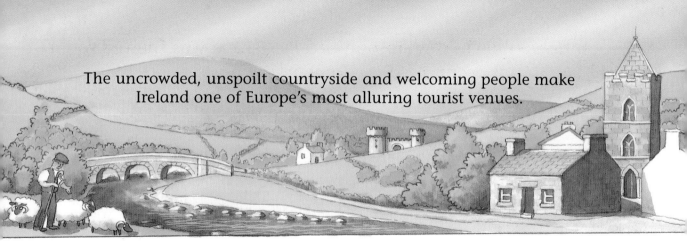

The uncrowded, unspoilt countryside and welcoming people make Ireland one of Europe's most alluring tourist venues.

Conflict between Catholics and Protestants has troubled Ulster for over 300 years. It flared sharply in 1969 and spilled over into the Irish Republic and Britain. Finally, in 1998 Unionists and Republicans accepted the Good Friday agreement that set out a formula for ending the conflict for ever.

In 1972 the people of the Irish Republic voted to join the European Economic Community (now the EU). By the 1990s, with EU assistance, the economy of the Irish Republic was one of the fastest growing in the world. National income more than doubled. The change was so fast and strong that the Republic earned the nickname 'The Celtic Tiger'.

There are more than 70 million people of Irish descent living around the world.

The first to leave were the missionary monks who travelled all over Europe. From the 17th century on many found their way to the New World. During the 19th century eight million men, women and children left – most to the USA, others to Britain and her colonies.

HAWAII HAS AN IRISH PIPE AND DRUMS FESTIVAL

IRISH PUBS ARE FOUND ALL OVER THE WORLD

SHAMROCK PUB,

DUBLINER'S INN, OSAKA

ST PATRICK'S DAY IS A BIGGER EVENT IN MANY NORTH AMERICAN CITIES THAN IN IRELAND

MANY OF EUROPE'S RAILWAYS WERE BUILT BY IRISH LABOUR.

O'MALLEY'S, SHANGHAI

GUINNESS 400,000 BARRELS SOLD EVERY YEAR IN U.S.A.

CANADA

MISSIONARIES IN EARLY CHRISTIAN TIMES IRISH MISSIONARIES GOT AS FAR AS KIEV IN THE UKRAINE

BETWEEN 1850–1930 4 MILLION IRISH WENT TO THE USA.

EMIGRATION IS NOT JUST A CHRONICLE OF SORROW AND REGRET. IT IS ALSO A POWERFUL STORY OF CONTRIBUTION AND ADAPTATION.

AT LEAST ONE THIRD OF ALL U.S. PRESIDENTS COULD CLAIM IRISH DESCENT. JOHN F. KENNEDY WAS THE FIRST CATHOLIC PRESIDENT, ELECTED IN 1960.

AUSTRALIA MANY IRISH SETTLED HERE. NED KELLY, THE FAMOUS OUTLAW, WAS FROM AN IRISH FAMILY

FORMER PRESIDENT MARY ROBINSON

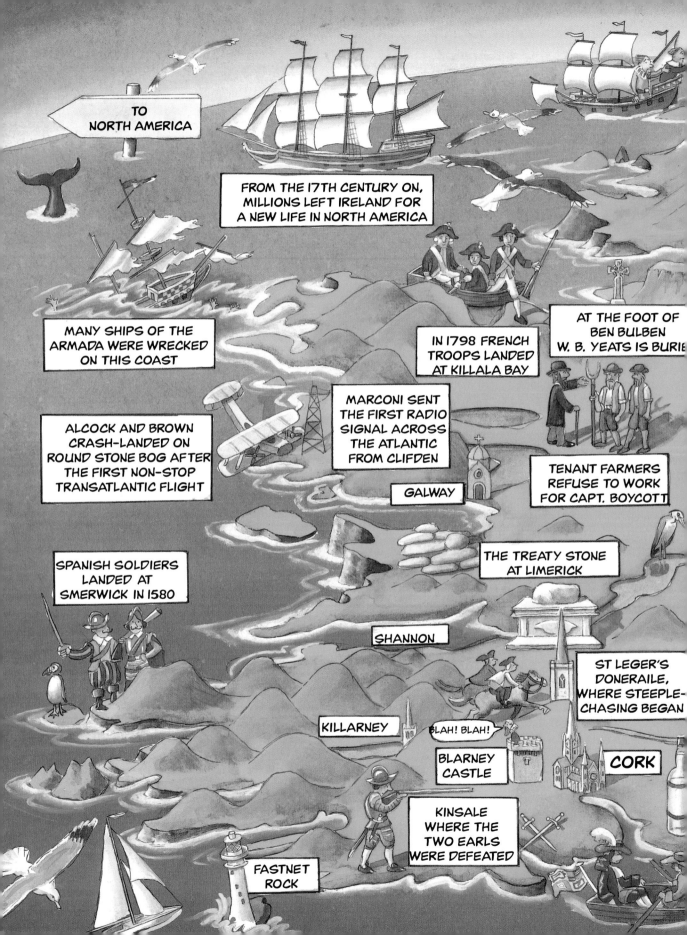